Christmas

 **W9-AWM-245**

From Kusy
To Karen & Jere

The Best
Golf Jokes
Ever

The Best Golf Jokes Ever

Bob Lonigan

BARNES
&NOBLE
BOOKS
NEW YORK

*For helping me with the jokes, cartoons, quotes,
stories, and advice on my golf grip, I want to
thank a number of people, including:*

*Brian Mackerer, Mike Mackerer, Kevin Charlton,
Bob Cook, Richard Binswanger, Tyler Russell,
Steve Taylor, Bill McIntosh, Bill Thompson,
Dr. Tim Charlton, and others too numerous to mention.*

"Putter."

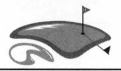

Mogridge was having a particularly bad day on the links. To make matters worse, his caddy had a horrible case of hiccups, which had lasted for several holes. Finally, on the 18th fairway, Mogridge drove his second shot into the middle of a lake. Furious, he began cursing out his caddy.

"That was all because of you and your damn hiccups," he screamed.

"But I didn't hiccup then," complained the caddy.

"That's the problem!" yelled Mogridge. "I ALLOWED for it!"

Balaban hit his first shot 250 yards, down the right side of the fairway, where it hit a rock and bounced into the woods. After finding the ball, he proceeded to slice his next shot off to the side, where it smacked into a tree, ricocheted back, and struck him in the forehead, killing him instantly. The next thing he knew, he was face to face with St. Peter at the pearly gates.

"Well, Balaban," intoned St. Peter. "I see you were an avid golfer. Is that correct?"

"Yes, it is," replied Balaban.

"Did you hit the ball a long way?" inquired St. Peter.

"Sure did," said Balaban proudly. "I got here in two, didn't I?"

"It is impossible to imagine Goethe or Beethoven being good at billiards or golf."

—H. L. Mencken

Two men were leaving church on a bright Sunday morning. "You know," said the first friend, "I can always tell who the golfers are in church."

"How's that?" asked his friend.

"It's easy," he said. "Just look at who is praying with an interlocking grip."

A foursome of golfers was searching for one of its golf balls that had landed in the deep rough. After several minutes of laboring, the golfer who had sliced the ball poked in the grass and declared, "I found it!"

One of the other golfers then screamed, "You liar! I have your ball in my pocket!"

"The fun you get from golf is in direct ratio to the effort you don't put into it."

—Bob Allen

"The place of the father in the modern suburban family is a very small one, particularly if he plays golf."

—Bertrand Russell

"He was born to be a golfer. He's color blind."

After being away from home for three months trying to make it on the European tour, Grimsby, a young golf pro, was finally home and in bed with his wife, hoping to make up for lost time. Later that evening they were both asleep, when a loud knock came at the door. They both sat up quickly, not realizing where they were.

"My God, that must be your husband!" exclaimed Grimsby, not yet fully awake.

"No, it can't be," said his wife. "He's in Europe playing golf."

"How did your doctor's appointment go?" asked Genifer when her husband walked in the house.

"Well, there's good news and there's bad news," he answered. "My blood pressure is too high, and I've got to lose about 25 pounds, the doctor told me. At his suggestion, I'm going to take up golf."

Genifer paused, "And the good news?"

Did you hear about the local country club that was determined to be politically correct? Instead of saying the golfers have handicaps, they say they're "stroke-challenged."

"What kind of nut would be out fishing in this weather?"

Harry, one of the club's poorer players, was out for his usual round of golf and was being attended to by a new teenage caddy. After hitting another poor shot, he decided to explain his situation to the youngster.

"You see, I recently took up golf to practice self-control," he said.

"Really?" replied the incredulous teenager. "In that case, you should have become a caddy."

Jones was obsessed by golf and thought and talked of nothing else, day after day, day in and day out. His wife, bless her soul, had put up with it for years, but she had almost reached her breaking point. Finally, one morning at breakfast, she snapped.

"Listen," she snarled. "Every day, all day, it's golf, golf, golf. Enough is enough. Just for a change, can we have a meal without talking about golf?"

"Why, sure," replied Jones, taken aback by her sudden outburst. "What should we talk about instead?"

"I really don't care," answered his wife with disgust. "Talk about sex."

"Okay," said Jones brightly. "Gee, I wonder who my new caddy is sleeping with?"

Bart, the club pro, was out for an afternoon of golf. He joined a group of three hackers who obviously were just beginners. After playing 15 brilliant holes, Bart had thoroughly impressed the novices, smacking every drive down the middle and hitting every green with his approach shots. Stepping up to the 16th tee, however, he angled his body away from the distant flag and drove his shot toward a road that ran along the side of the fairway. The ball bounced over the low fence and bounded onto the road just as a bus happened to be passing by. The bus hit the ball, knocking it back over the fence, where it bounced up onto the green. The group of novices was amazed.

"How in the world did you ever do that?" asked one of the awestruck golfers.

"Oh, it's easy," replied Bart, "as long as you know the bus schedule."

Fred had tried to be particularly careful about his language as he played golf with his preacher. But on the 12th hole, when he twice failed to hit out of a sand trap, he lost his resolve and let fly with a string of expletives. The preacher felt obliged to respond. "I have observed," he said in a calm voice, "that the best golfers do not use foul language."

"I guess not," said Fred. "What the hell do they have to cuss about?"

DEFINITIONS

Human rain delay—a slow player.

Red ass—murdering the next tee shot after just missing a short bogey putt on the previous hole.

Deploy the chute—what you yell at a putt that needs to slow down.

Write when you get work—spoken to a putt that has just run past the hole and is still going hard.

Mother-in-law putt—nothing but lip.

Lawrence of Arabia—someone who's been in the sand all day.

Army golf—left-right-left-right.

Linda Ronstadt drive—you hit a drive past your partners and say "blew by you."

Fore, Lord!—yelled after hitting a ball a mile in the air.

"If I don't make this next putt," said Ben, "I'm going to jump off a 100-foot cliff!"

"Aw," replied Stan, "that's just a big bluff."

Mike and Brian had just completed a round of golf and were relaxing with a couple of beers in the clubhouse bar. They had forgotten the frustrations of missed putts and shanked shots and were discussing all the reasons why they liked the game of golf.

"What I like about golf, Bri," said Mike, "is that you can spend the day outdoors walking around some beautiful countryside. You get a little exercise, some sun, and it takes your mind off troubles at work and at home."

"Forget about that," said Brian dismissively. "I'll tell you why golf is such a great game. Where else can you spend the day with a bunch of hookers and not have your wife kill you?!"

A grandfather and grandson were playing a round of golf together. The fourth hole was a difficult dogleg to the left, about 150 yards out from the tee. The grandson, hitting first, was planning on hitting his shot straight down the fairway when his grandfather said, "When I was your age, I'd aim right over those trees and hit the green every time. I'd never play it safe."

The grandson thought for a moment and then adjusted his stance to give it a try. He hit a perfect drive, but it hit the top of a 50-foot tree and dropped down. He looked silently at his shot.

As the grandfather teed up his ball he paused, "Of course, when I was your age, those trees were just eight feet tall."

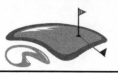

"Take him with you dear. He loves to play in the sand too."

The police arrived and found a woman dead on her living-room floor with a golf club next to her body.

One of them asked the husband, "Mr. Jones, is this your wife?"

"Yes," the distraught man replied.

"Did you kill her?" a policeman asked.

"Yes, I did," he sighed.

After examining the body, Sergeant Flaherty said, "It looks to me like you struck her eight times with this 3-iron. Is that correct?"

"I'm afraid it is," Jones admitted, "but put me down for a 5."

Three duffers were golfing with the club pro. The first duffer teed off and hit a dribbler about 60 yards. He turned to the pro and asked, "What did I do wrong?"

The pro replied, "Loft."

The next duffer teed off and duck-hooked into the woods. He asked the pro the same question.

The pro again answered, "Loft."

The third teed off and sliced into a pond. He too asked the pro, "What did I do wrong?"

Again, "Loft."

As they were walking down the fairway, the first duffer finally spoke up to the pro. "All three of us hit completely different tee shots and yet when we asked you what we did wrong, you gave the same exact answer each time. So what is 'loft?'"

The pro shook his head. "Lack of Fricking Talent."

Monroe had just played one of the worst rounds of golf of his life. As he trudged back to the clubhouse, feeling sorry for himself, he said to his caddy, "Well, caddy, I guess I'm just about the worst golfer in the whole wide world."

"Oh, no, sir," replied his caddy, "There are a lot worse than you. It's just that they don't play."

A man named Myers was playing alone behind a threesome of women. It was a busy weekend, and the play was slow. When Myers got to the next tee the three women were about to hit, and he asked them if he might join them in order to speed up play. They all agreed that it was a good idea. All four got off good drives and walked out to hit their second shots. The three women hit nice iron shots safely onto the green. But Myers put his into a bunker next to the green and promptly swore, "@#$%&Y&!" One of the women heard him and was outraged and told him that they would not tolerate any profanity. Myers apologized, and the foursome finished out the hole.

When they got to the next tee the woman who scolded him hooked her tee shot. At first it looked like it would just end up in the light rough, but it hit a tree, and bounded into the woods. "@#$%&Y&!" she yelled, and stormed off to search for the ball.

Upon hearing the expletive, Myers stared at the woman and said, "I thought you wouldn't tolerate that type of language."

She turned to him and snarled, "Yeah, but your ball didn't hit a @#$%&Y& tree!"

"The only shots you can be dead sure of are those you've had already."

—*Byron Nelson*

17

Did you hear about the golfer who was condemned to die by hanging? He asked the hangman, "Mind if I take a few practice swings?"

It was the midsummer dance at the venerable old golf club, and Woodruff, the venerable old head of the rules committee, wandered out on the patio to get away from the music. Thinking he heard giggling and other sounds coming from the 18th green, he made his way over to investigate. Peering down into the large sand trap abutting the green, he saw a young couple laughing and rolling around, various articles of clothing strewn about.

"I say there, what's going on?" demanded Woodruff of the couple.

Startled, the two shrieked, grabbed their clothes up, and sprinted out of the sand trap, across the fairway, and disappeared into the trees.

Woodruff was joined a minute later by another gentleman who had popped out to smoke a cigarette, and who had seen the two run off.

"Were those two members, Woodruff?" he asked.

"Certainly not," Woodruff replied in a huff. "If they were they would have raked the trap."

"I'd show it to you, but your father taped a
golf tournament over our wedding video."

"Lay off for three weeks, and then quit for good."

—*Sam Snead*

While driving his cart across the course, a club golf pro came upon a young woman golfer whom he had never seen before. She had a puzzled look on her face, so he asked her what was wrong. She replied, "Well, this is the first time I have ever been golfing, and I shot a 66."

The pro couldn't believe it. After a few speechless moments, he said to her, "That is a wonderful score. You should be very proud."

But the woman was unconvinced and replied, "Maybe you're right, but I am hoping to do a little better on the next hole."

Joe, Jack, Bill, and Bob approached the 15th green and marked their balls. All of a sudden, Bill fell to the ground. The others rushed to him, and all three hovered over him. After a minute a terrific fight broke out among the three. A lone golfer standing nearby ran over and eventually separated the trio.

"What in the world's the matter?" he asked in wonder.

"Well, you see," began Bob, "my partner over there just had a stroke and died."

"Why, that's horrible," gasped the Samaritan. "But why in the world were you fighting?"

"Well," explained Bob, "these other two bozos want to include the stroke in his score!"

"I can't see it lasting very long."

Roderick was in the middle of a round of golf at her country club. As she shanked shot after shot, her poor play made the round torture for her caddy to watch. After Roderick's third shot on the 11th hole left her still 180 yards from the green, she turned to her caddy and asked, "Do you think I can get there with a 5-iron?"

"Oh sure, Mrs. Roderick," replied her caddy. "Eventually!"

S.GROSS

Millie, Mavis, and Marian were having tea at a local golf club. When Millie returned to the table after a visit to the ladies' room, she reported that a small hole in the wall of the facilities allowed a person to look right into the men's locker room. The three women decided to go examine the situation.

Peering through the hole, Millie saw a man taking a shower. His head, however, was cut off from view. Millie chuckled and said, "I don't know who that is, but it sure isn't my husband!"

Mavis was the next one to take a look. "I don't know who he is either," she replied, "but he definitely isn't my husband!"

Marian now took a look. "I don't know who he is either," she reported. "But not only isn't he my husband, he's not even a member of the club!"

As they approached the first tee, Sally and Ann were all set for a relaxing round of golf. Sally reached into her bag to get a ball.

"Why don't you try this ball?" asked her friend, holding out a red ball. "You can't possibly lose it."

"What do you mean, you can't lose it? I can lose any ball," replied Ann.

"Not this one," assured Sally. "If you hit it into the woods, it makes a beeping sound so you know where it is. If you hit it into the water, it gives off a gas that makes bubbles so you can find it. If you hit it in the fairway, it produces smoke so you can see it. And if you hit it into a sand trap, it's easy to see because of its red color."

Ann didn't quite believe her friend, but over the next couple of holes, Sally showed her all the possibilities and she finally became convinced.

"That ball really is amazing!" said Ann. "Where did you ever get it?"

"Oh, I found it."

Bumper sticker: "Under par is when I run out of holes before I run out of balls."

23

"You're a sadistic psychopath who enjoys inflicting misery on others, Mr. Winslow. You'd be a terrific golf-course designer."

"Congratulate me!" exclaimed Mildred. "I broke 80 today!"

"How terrific!" gushed her friend Joan. "That's a lot of clubs for one day!"

GOLF IS . . .

twenty percent mechanics and technique. The other 80 percent is philosophy, humor, tragedy, romance, melodrama, companionship, camaraderie, cussedness, and conversation.

—Grantland Rice

based on honesty. Where else would you admit to a 7 on a par 3?

—Jimmy Demaret

a game where guts and blind devotion will always net you absolutely nothing but an ulcer.

—Tommy Bolt

easy. You just swing the club and say, "Oh, no . . . no!"

—Unknown

a game that needlessly prolongs the lives of some of our most useless citizens.

—Bob Hope

"Is golf really a sport, in all honesty? I thought in a sport you had to run at some point."

—John McEnroe

A couple whose passion had cooled went to a marriage counselor for advice. They went through a number of sessions with little success, until suddenly at one session the counselor grabbed the wife and kissed her passionately.

"There," he said to the husband. "That's what she needs every Monday, Wednesday, Saturday, and Sunday."

"Well," replied the husband, "I can bring her in on Mondays and Wednesdays, but Saturdays and Sundays are my golf days."

"Let's see, I think right now I'm third in the money-winning and first in money-spending."

—Tony Lema

"The harder you work, the luckier you get."

—Gary Player

"The difference between golf and tennis is that tennis is murder—you just want to kill the other player. Golf is suicide—you just want to kill yourself. Tennis is like a wonderful, long-standing relationship with a husband. Golf is a tempestuous, lousy lover; it's totally unpredictable, a constant surprise."

—Dinah Shore

26

"It looks to me like they come in peace."

"No one who ever had lessons would have a swing like mine."

—*Lee Trevino*

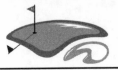

PHILOSOPHY

- The man who takes up golf to get his mind off work soon takes up work to get his mind off golf.

- The secret to good golf is to hit the ball hard, straight, and not too often.

- There are three ways to improve your golf score: take lessons, practice often, or start cheating.

- The best way to improve your golf is to take it up at an earlier age.

- The less skilled a player is, the more likely he is to give you tips.

- If golf is good exercise, why isn't mowing the lawn?

- Real golfers don't miss putts, they get robbed.

- Real golfers have two handicaps: one for bragging and one for betting.

- Sunday is the day that many men bow their heads. Some are in church, but the majority are out playing golf.

Woodruff had just bought a new set of expensive woods and set to use them for the first time. After playing one of his worst rounds ever, he returned to the pro shop where he had purchased the clubs.

"How do you like the clubs?" asked the pro.

"Oh, just great," replied Woodruff, sarcastically. "These are the best clubs I've ever played with. In fact, I can throw these at least 40 yards farther than my old ones!"

"The players themselves can be classified into two groups—the attractions and the entry fees."
—*Jimmy Demaret*

Hogan's wife was furious when he walked in the door with a brand new set of golf clubs.

"And just where did you get those?" she demanded.

"Don't worry, dear," he replied, "they didn't cost me a cent."

"Really?" she asked. "How's that?"

"Well," said Hogan, "They were marked down from $600 to $300, so I bought them with the $300 I saved!"

Dunne and Broadstreet were out playing golf and were approaching the third tee. Just as Dunne was about to tee off, a beautiful naked woman ran past him. He was distracted for a few seconds but, as any true golfer would, he put his head back down and concentrated on the task at hand. Again, he was about to hit his shot, when suddenly two men in white coats raced past. Once more he was distracted but again managed to control himself. He prepared to hit for a third time, when another man in a white coat rushed past, this one carrying a bucket of sand in each hand.

Eventually, Dunne managed to put this third distraction behind him and hit his drive down the fairway. Broadstreet followed with his shot, and as the two men walked after their balls Dunne said, "I wonder what in the world all that was about."

"Oh, I can explain," said Broadstreet. "You see, that woman is an inmate at the mental institution across the road. Once a week or so, she manages to escape. She tears off all her clothes and runs across the fairways on the course. The three guys running after her are nurses. They have a race to see who can catch her. The one who wins gets to carry her back."

"I see, but what about the guy with the buckets of sand?"

"Oh, that guy won last week," explained Broadstreet. "The buckets of sand are his handicap."

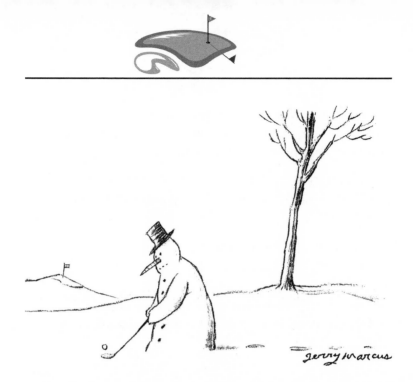

Two hackers and their caddies were searching for a ball that had been sliced into the rough. Poking around in the brush, the first hacker looked over at his partner and yelled, "What sort of ball is it?"

Before the other hacker could answer, his caddy piped up, "A brand new one. It hasn't been properly hit yet."

"I'm in the woods so much I can tell you which plants are edible."

—*Lee Trevino*

While awaiting their tee time, Barry and John were having coffee. Barry showed John some new, expensive golf balls that he had just purchased.

"You know, I think the caddy I've been assigned is a thief," Barry said. "I'm afraid he's going to swipe these new balls."

"I wouldn't putt it past him."

"So how come Emily took up golf?" asked Doreen.

"Oh, her brother told her about a woman finding a diamond in the rough!"

Leslie was a complete neophyte at golf, but she decided to play in her company's annual golf outing. She was assigned to a foursome, and when her turn came to tee off she emulated the others and took a mighty swing. Somehow she connected, and the ball went soaring high, landing on the edge of the green and rolling in for a hole in one.

After her partners congratulated her and finished playing the hole, they all walked to the second tee. When it was her turn, Leslie closed her eyes, took a big swing, and connected squarely. Again, the ball rose high and far, landing on the green, and rolling into the cup.

Leslie breathed an audible sigh of relief. "Whew, I thought I had missed it this time."

The rich American duffer had just finished bashing his way around venerable St. Andrews Golf Club in Scotland and was having a drink at the bar. The secretary of the club stopped to speak with the bartender, and when he finished the American asked him a question.

"I've got a box of Cuban cigars and a spare bottle of single-malt whisky," he said. "What do you think I should give to my caddy as a present?"

The secretary checked the American's card, sighed, and replied, "Your clubs!"

"I'm going to win so much money this year, my caddy will make the top twenty money-winners list."

—*Lee Trevino*

An American playing golf in Scotland for the first time was having the worst round of his life. Not happy about it, he groused to his caddy, "These are terrible links, Angus, worst I've ever seen."

"I'm very sorry, Mr. Lippincott, but these aren't links," Angus replied. "We got off them about an hour ago."

"How do you like my game, caddy?" Arnold asked proudly.

"It's okay, sir, but I still prefer golf."

Robbins, a newcomer to the sport, was playing his first round of golf. He had hired the pro to go around with him and give him a few pointers. On the par 3 first tee, Robbins asked, "So what do I do now?"

The pro scratched his head at the question and replied, "Well, see that flag way out there on the green? You have to hit your ball as close to it as you can."

Robbins wound up, made a mighty swing, and connected squarely. The ball went flying, eventually coming to rest three inches from the hole.

Robbins looked around at the pro. "What do I do now?"

The pro looked at Robbins in surprise and answered, "You are supposed to hit it in the hole."

Robbins opened his mouth and screamed, "Why didn't you tell me that before!"

Two acquaintances were having lunch and discussing their golf games.

"Do you play much golf each week?" asked Smith.

"Oh, about 36 holes, roughly speaking," replied Dwoinen.

"And how many without cursing?" asked Smith.

Louis, an avid golfer, married Selma, but soon the marriage began having problems because Louis insisted on playing golf five times a week. They finally sat down to talk about it with a counselor, who asked Louis if he would teach Selma how to play golf. That way, they could both enjoy the game and have something in common that would improve their marriage. But Louis was hesitant. "Golf is a serious game," he said. "She only wants to do this to make fun of it."

After some discussion back and forth, Louis finally agreed to let Selma come to the course with him.

The next day, they went to the club, and Selma signed up for some lessons with the pro. The lessons continued every day, and Louis was happy because his wife was finally off his back.

One day, his friend Sam approached him in the clubhouse.

"How's your marriage going?" asked Sam.

"Great," replied Louis. "Ever since my wife has been taking lessons, she leaves me alone and lets me play all the golf I want."

"I see," answered Sam. "Then I guess you don't know that she's been fooling around with the golf pro."

Louis's eyes turned red with anger and steam could be seen coming out of his ears.

"I knew it," he screamed. "I knew that sooner or later she'd make a mockery of the game!"

A schoolteacher was taking her first golf lesson.

"Is the word spelled P-U-T-T or P-U-T?" she asked the club pro.

"P-U-T-T is correct," he replied. "'Put' means to place something where you want it. 'Putt' means to make a vain attempt to do the same thing."

For the past 25 years Benson had worked as an accountant for very old and very rich Mr. Tipton. The elderly gentleman realized that his time was growing short and decided to reward his loyal employee for his many years of service. He asked Benson what he would like.

"A set of golf clubs would be nice," replied the accountant. The rich man asked Benson how many clubs are in a set.

"Fourteen," Benson replied.

About a month went by, and the accountant began to have second thoughts. Perhaps he should have just asked for a watch or something easier to find.

Finally, one day, Mr. Tipton called. "I have some good news and some bad news," said the old man. "The good news is that I managed to get you ten clubs. The bad news is that only seven of them have swimming pools."

The pope met with the college of cardinals to discuss a proposal from Shimon Peres, the former leader of Israel.

"Your Holiness," began one of the cardinals, "Mr. Peres would like to devise a method for seeing which of our peoples is more athletic. He has challenged us to a golf match to decide the question. He wants us to send one of the leaders of the church to play one of their leaders."

The pontiff was somewhat reluctant, but eventually agreed to the match. "But who will be our representative?" he asked.

The cardinal smiled. "Don't worry," he assured the pope. "I have a plan. We'll call America and talk to the great golfer Jack Nicklaus. We'll make him a cardinal and then he'll be able to play for our side. We can't lose!"

Everyone thought it was a splendid plan, and the call was placed to Jack Nicklaus. Nicklaus was honored and agreed to play.

The big day came, and the two representatives met for the match. Following the round of golf, Nicklaus called the Vatican to talk to the pope.

"I played very well, Your Holiness," he said. "In fact, I lost by only one stroke."

The pope was shocked. "You lost?" he exclaimed. "You came in second to Shimon Peres?"

"Not to Shimon Peres," said Nicklaus. "I lost to Rabbi Woods."

"I carry my clubs like this because it drives Fred crazy."

"I enjoy shooting in the 120s. I figure I'm getting more for my money."

—*Bill McIntosh*

Boggle was playing a round of golf with three of his buddies and not doing especially well. On the 12th hole, which bordered a lake, he proceeded to hit seven balls into the water. Frustrated over his poor play, he heaved his clubs into the water and began to walk off the course. About 50 yards away, however, he abruptly turned around, walked to the lake, and jumped in.

"I knew he'd change his mind," said one friend. "Now he's gone back to retrieve his clubs."

When Boggle emerged from the water, however, he didn't have his clubs with him. Again, to the puzzlement of his friends, he began to walk off the course.

"Hey, Boggle," yelled one of them, "how come you jumped back into the water?"

"Harrumph," snorted Boggle. "I left my car keys in the bag."

At a local golf club, the women members had been monopolizing the practice tees as well as the regular course. A couple of angry husbands decided to take matters into their own hands. They begin to deliberately aim their drives at the women, taking care not to actually hit them. This dangerous practice finally caused the greens committee to post a warning: "Drive carefully. The wife you shave may be your own!"

QUESTIONS

Q: Why did the golfer bring two pairs of shoes with him?

A: In case he got a hole in one.

Q: What's the difference between a golfer and a fisherman?

A: When a golfer lies, he doesn't have to bring anything home to prove it.

Q: Why was Adolph Hitler the worst golfer in history?

A: He never made it out of the bunker.

Q: What are the four worst words you could hear during a round of golf?

A: It's still your turn.

Q: What's the difference between a bad golfer and a skydiver?

A: A bad golfer goes "whack, . . . damn!" A skydiver goes "damn, . . . whack!"

Sandberg was fed up with his caddy snickering at each shot he took, and finally lashed out.

"That's it. I'm sick and tired of your insolence. As soon as this round is over, I'm going to report you to the caddy master."

"Hee hee," chortled the caddy. "I'll be an old man by then."

"If you want to take long walks, take long walks. If you want to hit things with a stick, hit things with a stick. But there's no excuse for combining the two and putting the results on TV. Golf is not so much a sport as an insult to lawns."

—National Lampoon

While he was out of town on a long business trip, Haggerty decided to take a day off and play golf. Since he was a stranger, he figured he would be paired up with a partner at the course. When he arrived there, he discovered there were no men waiting to go on, but there was a very beautiful blonde named Marlene waiting to play. At the suggestion of the club pro, Haggerty decided to pair up with Marlene.

After playing 17 holes together, Haggerty and Marlene got to know each other quite well. By the time they walked up to the 18th tee, they were both equally frustrated with their game.

41

As luck would have it, both got off good drives on the par 4 18th, and both reached the green with their second shot. Haggerty, away at 35 feet, saw his chance to finish out on a high note with a birdie. His hopes soaring, he turned to Marlene and said, "If I make this shot, I'll buy us dinner tonight!"

He hit his ball, and it rolled down the gently sloping green, and, amazingly, dropped into the cup for a birdie. Haggerty was elated.

Not to be outdone, Marlene approached her ball and lined it up. Certain that she didn't have a chance in the world of sinking the twisting 30-footer, she smiled at Haggerty and said, "If I make this shot, I'll invite you back to my place for drinks after dinner."

Haggerty's eyes lit up. "Wait!" he said. "Let me help you line up the putt."

He walked over to where her ball was and picked it up. "That's a gimme if I ever saw one."

Johnson made an awful swing and tore up a large divot. She picked up the nearly square-foot of turf and, looking back at her caddy, asked, "What shall I do with this?"

"If I were you," advised the caddy, "I'd take it home to practice on."

Brixton and Batton were out for a pleasant afternoon of golf. Brixton addressed the ball, took a tremendous swing, and sent the ball slicing away into the distance. The ball flew into an adjacent fairway where it hit a man full-force on the head. The man dropped to the ground as if shot. Horrified, Brixton and Batton ran to where the man lay unconscious, with the ball resting between his feet.

"This is horrible!" exclaimed Brixton. "What should I do?"

"Don't move him!" yelled her partner. "If we leave him here, he becomes an immovable obstruction and you can either play the ball as it lies or drop it two club lengths away!"

"Rule number one: Never laugh!"

Mr. Wong, a Chinese businessman, was visiting his newly acquired business in the United States. As a gesture of goodwill, the executives of the company took him to a local country club for a round of golf, which Mr. Wong had never played or seen before. Upon his return to his native land, Mr. Wong's family asked him what his trip was like.

"Very interesting," replied the elderly businessman. "I played a new game. Hit a little white ball with a long stick in a big cow pasture. Name of the game is 'Oh, Damn!'"

44

Father John was a parish priest, and an avid golfer in his free time. He was teaching a Sunday school class about Jesus' ability to answer difficult questions. Father Sebastian, Father John's golfing partner, happened to be outside the door, anxiously waiting to hit the links.

". . . so when Jesus was writing in the sand," said Father John, "the Pharisees sought to trap him in his words."

"Aha!" said Father Sebastian. "Even Jesus had difficulty with sand traps!"

Four old golfing buddies were walking down the fairway toward the 16th green.

"These hills are getting steeper and steeper every year," groaned Blimey.

"And these fairways seem to be getting longer and longer, too," added Barton.

"And these sand traps seem to be bigger than I remember them, also," sighed Oswald.

"Hey, quit your complaining," said Dickson, the oldest of the four. "Just be thankful we're still on the right side of the grass."

"Relax? How can anybody relax and play golf? You have to grip the club don't you?"

—*Ben Hogan*

DEFINITIONS

Amateur golfer—someone who addresses the ball twice: once before swinging, and once again after swinging.

Oxymoron—an easy par three.

A hack—when your divot flies farther than your ball.

Bad golfer—someone who can take strokes off his game only with an eraser.

Duffer—the only guy in the world who has an unplayable lie when he tees up.

Life is a beach—hit into a sand trap.

Dolly Parton—a putt that uses all of the cup before falling into the hole.

NBA 3-pointer—shot holed out on the fly.

Lunar landscape—unrepaired ball marks on green.

Getting your money's worth—many strokes.

Bleached skull—ball in the sand.

Mexican hat dance—lots of spike marks around the hole.

In jail—deep in the trees with no shot out.

Worm burner—a shot going a long way on the ground.

"If I had my way, any man guilty of golf would be ineligible for any office of trust in the United States."

—*H. L. Mencken*

Ahmed and Roberts were living it up at a sales meeting, drunk out of their minds, the night before a big company golf match. The next day, against all odds, the pair managed to stay even with their opponents through 17 holes. On the 18th, by some miracle, they were in position to win the match. All that had to happen was for one of them to sink his seven-foot putt.

Roberts lined up his seven-footer, taking his spread-eagle stance with his feet wide apart. Just as he drew his putter back, a large black dog came bounding out of the woods and ran across the green, right between Roberts's legs. Roberts never even flinched. He putted the ball with a firm stroke and it went right in the middle of the hole for the win.

Ahmed was ecstatic. "That was unbelievable!" he shouted. "I've never seen such total concentration before in my life. How in the world did you ever manage to drop that putt with that dog running between your legs?"

"Oh," exclaimed Roberts, "you mean that was a real dog?"

"You don't know what pressure is until you've played for five dollars with only two in your pocket."

—*Lee Trevino*

One day, a young man was out golfing with three friends. While approaching the fourth tee and walking behind his friends, he happened to look up and see what appeared to be some sort of demon in human clothing.

"Hey, you," said the demon. "How would you like to make every man's dream—a hole in one?"

"Sure, I would," said the man suspiciously, "but what's the catch?"

"Nothing much," assured the demon. "It will just shorten your sex life by five years."

The young man thought for a couple of seconds, then agreed. He teed his ball up, set himself, then proceeded to hit the best shot of his life. It flew straight down the middle of the fairway, bounced up onto the green, and rolled right into the cup. A hole in one! His friends were ecstatic.

The man was thrilled and began walking to the next tee. Again, the demon appeared by his side.

"How'd you like to make it two holes in one in a row?" he asked the man. "It's only been done five times in history."

"What will it cost me this time?" asked the man.

"It will shorten your sex life by another 20 years," answered the demon.

Again, the young man thought for a moment, then agreed to the condition. He teed his ball up, took his swing, and drove the sphere 225 yards down the middle of the fairway. Once again, the ball took a couple of big bounces onto the green, then rolled its way directly into the hole. His friends were amazed. He had made two successive holes in one.

The foursome approached the sixth tee, and a crowd began to gather around the group. For a third time, the demon came up next to the young man and whispered in his ear.

"Look," he said, "another hole in one would mean three in a row. It's never been done in the history of the world. How would you like to be the one to do it?"

"Sure," said the young man, thrilled with the attention he was receiving. "What do I have to give up this time?"

"You may never touch a person of the opposite sex ever again for the rest of your life," said the demon.

"Okay!" agreed the man. He teed up his ball and hit his shot 300 yards right down the center of the fairway. The ball took one big hop, bounded up on the green, then bounced right into the middle of the cup for his third hole in one in a row!

And that's how Father Mahoney got his name into the *Guinness Book of World Records*.

Tiger Woods and Stevie Wonder were sitting in a bar discussing their work.

"How is your singing career going?" asked Woods.

"Not bad," replied Wonder. "My latest album has just gone platinum, so life couldn't be better. How's your golf game?"

"Pretty good," answered Woods. "I won four tournaments last year, though to tell you the truth, I'm having some problems with my swing that still need to be straightened out."

"Whenever my swing goes wrong," Wonder replied, "I find that I need to get away from golf for a while. The next time I play, it usually seems to come back."

Woods was taken aback. "You play golf?" he asked.

"Sure," said Wonder. "I've been playing it for years."

"But you're blind," said Woods. "How can you play golf if you're blind?"

"Easy," replied the singer. "I make my caddy stand in the middle of the fairway and call out to me. I listen for the sound of his voice, then swing in his direction. We repeat this until I'm on the green."

"But how do you putt?" asked Woods.

"I have my caddy lean down in front of the hole, put his head to the ground, and call to me. I putt to the sound of his voice."

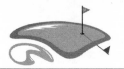

"There's no such thing as a 'gimme.'"

"Wow!" said Woods. "We'll have to get together and play a round sometime."

"Sure thing," answered Wonder. "But to tell you the truth, most people don't take me seriously, so I only play for money. And never less than $10,000 a hole."

After thinking for a moment, Woods said, "Okay, I'm up for that. When do you want to play?"

"It really doesn't matter," replied Wonder. "Any night next week is fine with me."

A Martian spaceship containing two aliens, Blat and Splat, hovered over a golf course while the pair observed a lone neophyte golfer. They watched as the beginner dribbled her tee shot then shanked her second shot into the rough. She managed to get out of the rough and onto the fairway, but her next shot put her in a bunker near the green. It took her three shots to get out of the trap, and then three more putts before finally holing her ball. After watching her round with fascination, Blat turned to Splat and said, "Wow! Now she's really in serious trouble!"

A beautiful blonde golfer went into the pro shop and looked around. Frowning, she finally went up to the desk.

"Do you have any green golf balls?" she asked.

The pro scratched his head, looked all over the shop, then began searching through several catalogs, but all to no avail. There were no green golf balls. The blonde started toward the door in disgust, but before she left, the pro asked, "Could you tell me why you want green golf balls?"

Giving him a look of disdain, the blonde replied, "Well, obviously, they would be much easier to find in the sand traps!"

"Putts get real difficult the day they hand out the money."

—*Lee Trevino*

For several months, the team of archaeologists had been hard at work deep in the Amazon jungle, clearing away underbrush as they searched for evidence of the Lost City. Finally, their efforts appeared to be bearing fruit. They began to uncover what seemed to be large, wide, winding avenues of giant flagstones. Every few hundred yards, they found deep, perfectly circular holes dug into the ground. Amazingly, it appeared that they had come across nothing less than an ancient golf course. Their guess was corroborated when they found drawings of human figures using primitive clubs and balls.

The archaeologists decided to interview the elders of the local Indian tribe to see if there were any traditions associated with the ancient course. It turned out that the tribe had legends about the Old Ones, who had followed a daily ritual involving clubs and balls. Unfortunately, some tragedy seemed to have occurred and put an end to the ritual.

Watching one of the elders speaking with an interpreter, one of the archaeologists mused out loud, "If only we knew why they stopped playing."

Turning to the interpreter, she said, "Could you ask him what made the Old Ones give up this activity?" The interpreter nodded and relayed the question to the elder. The elder listened intently to him, then with a smile and a wave of his hand, he gave his answer.

"Simple," said the interpreter. "They couldn't afford the greens fees."

SAID TO YOUR PARTNER

Pitching wood—said to your partner when he skies his drive.

First day with the new hands?—said to your partner after he hits a particularly bad chip.

Hit a 3-wood— said to your partner when he's got a really long putt.

Run it out—said to your partner after he pops up off the tee.

Got your putter stuck in your bra—said to your partner when he leaves a putt off line.

One in a row—said to your partner when he finally hits a decent shot.

A little light in the loafers—said to your partner when he leaves a putt short.

This course is hard—said to your partner when he whiffs on a shot.

We knew there was a hole somewhere—said to your partner when he finally sinks a putt.

Gargle peanut butter—said to your partner when he chokes.

Houston, we have a problem—said to your partner after he hits a very high tee shot.

*"Charlie just came in all excited.
He bowled a hole in one or something."*

Mr. Grandison, the oldest member of the golf club,
ambled into the clubhouse and began complaining.

"I can't get up out of the bunkers as well as I once
did," he lamented.

"I have one suggestion, Mr. Grandison," said the club
pro. "You could try opening up your club face a little
more."

"Oh, no," replied Mr. Grandison. "It's not the ball that's
giving me problems. I just can't get myself out."

Dunphy and Hill were playing golf one afternoon. They approached the eighth tee, which had a pond running alongside the fairway. Dunphy teed up his ball and promptly hooked it into the water. He reached into his bag but found he had no balls remaining.

"Excuse me, Hill," he said to his friend. "Can I borrow one of your balls?"

Hill agreed, and handed a ball to Dunphy. Dunphy took his second drive and again hooked it into the pond. This went on three more times, with exactly the same result.

After Dunphy had hit five balls into the water, Hill was getting a little bit annoyed at his friend. When Dunphy asked for another ball, Hill was hesitant.

"You know, Dunphy," said Hill, "these Titleists cost me a lot of money."

"Really?" replied Dunphy. "Well, if you can't afford to play the game, you really shouldn't be out here!"

Collier came upon his friend Reinsdorf, who was sitting at the club bar stirring a drink and looking morose. "What's the matter?" Collier asked.

"My doctor says I can't play golf any more," answered Reinsdorf, dejectedly.

"Oh," said Collier, "I see he's played with you too, huh?"

It was a bright, sunny morning and duffer Phil was on the first tee, beginning his routine, visualizing his upcoming shot. Suddenly, a voice over the clubhouse loudspeaker said, "Attention please! Will the man on the women's tee please back up to the men's tee."

Ignoring the interruption, Phil continued his routine, concentrating on his next shot. Again the voice boomed out, "Attention please! Will the man on the women's tee please back up to the men's tee!"

Enough was enough, thought Phil. "Attention!" he shouted back. "Will the announcer in the clubhouse please shut up and let the man play his second shot!"

Two beginners, Marilyn and Gretchen, were at the first hole of the local public links. Both had taken lessons, but this was their first time playing on a course. Marilyn, hitting first, shut her eyes and swung. She hit it straight and true and the ball soared high before it landed on the green and rolled into the hole.

"You just made a hole in one," Gretchen said in awe.

"Well, that wasn't so hard," said Marilyn. "I'll bet I can do it again before we're through."

"I'll bet you on that," replied Gretchen, "on one condition."

"Oh, what's that?"

"You've got to swing with your eyes open!"

*"I think your father keeps working just so he can
leave at three o'clock every day."*

Mr. and Mrs. Phillips were out enjoying a leisurely round of golf. Mrs. Phillips was about to tee off at the fourth hole. She swung and hit the ball, which sliced toward a row of expensive houses bordering the fairway. The ball headed directly toward a large plate-glass window, and, as they watched in horror, the ball smashed through the window, shattering it into a million shards of glass.

Guiltily, the couple walked toward the house to see the extent of the damage. They rang the doorbell, but no one answered. They peeked inside the broken window and saw a gentleman seated on a couch in the living room. He had what looked like a turban on his head.

Peering in through the broken window, Mrs. Phillips asked, "Do you live here?"

"No," replied the gentleman. "Someone must have just hit a ball through the window, which knocked over that vase. The vase broke, freeing me from that little bottle."

"My wife hit the ball," said Mr. Phillips.

"I am ever so grateful," said the man.

"Are you a genie?" ventured Mrs. Phillips.

"Yes, I am," he replied. "In fact, I am so grateful, I will grant you two wishes. If you don't mind, I will keep the third for myself."

"Sure," said the couple in unison, happy to have the chance to make the best of what could have been a bad situation.

The couple agreed on two wishes. First, they wanted an income of $1,000,000 a year for the rest of their lives. Secondly, Mr. Phillips wanted to have a scratch handicap.

"Done!" cried the genie.

"Now," he continued, turning to Mr. Phillips, "it's my turn. I have been locked up inside that bottle without any female companionship for many centuries. For my wish, I would like to have my way with your wife. I know it's a lot to ask, but remember, I made you a scratch golfer, and you're both millionaires."

There was a moment's hesitation, but the couple agreed. Mr. Phillips left to finish his game, and the genie and Mrs. Phillips repaired to the bedroom.

Two hours later, after making passionate love, the two were getting dressed. The genie turned to Mrs. Phillips and asked, "How long have you two been married?"

"Ten years" was her reply.

"And how old is your husband?"

"Thirty-three" was her answer.

The genie mulled this over. "Tell me," he asked, "how long has he believed in this genie stuff?"

Peebles, Williams, and Menze, avid golfers all their lives, were met by St. Peter at the gates of heaven. St. Peter explained that, inside the gates, heaven was home to the most magnificent, beautiful golf courses they could ever imagine. He told them they would each be given a set of golf clubs based on how faithful they had been to their spouses during their lives.

Peebles, the first to step up, confessed to St. Peter. "I'm sorry to have to admit it," he said, "but I cheated on my wife twice while we were married."

St. Peter reprimanded Peebles, saying it was a bad thing he had done. Then he gave him a middle-of-the-line set of golf clubs.

Williams was next. "I'm also sorry to have to admit it," he said, "I also cheated on my wife, but only once."

St. Peter admonished him, saying it was a bad thing he had done. Since he had done it only once, however, he received a better set of golf clubs.

Finally, it was Menze's turn. "I'm proud to say," he related, "I never once cheated on my wife."

St. Peter was very pleased. Since Menze had never cheated, St. Peter gave him an expensive set of Big Bertha™ oversized clubs and irons.

A couple of days later, Peebles and Williams were about to tee off at the first hole when they noticed Menze, with his Big Bertha™ clubs, sitting on a bench near the side of the fairway, crying his eyes out.

"What's the matter?" asked Peebles, approaching him. "You got the best set of clubs. What are you crying about?"

"Well, I just saw my wife coming off the 18th green," explained Menze. "All she was carrying was a 7-iron and a putter."

A genie, who had been playing behind a foursome of duffers all day, hit his drive about 250 yards right down the middle of the fairway. Unfortunately, the ball took a big bounce and hit Plinkton, one of the duffers, right in the head. The genie rushed to Plinkton's side to see if she was hurt. Standing over the stricken golfer, the genie said, "I'm terribly sorry I hit you with my shot, but since I'm a genie I will grant you one wish to try to make it up to you. What would you like?"

Plinkton rubbed her head for a moment or two, then said, "Well, I've always wanted to go to Hawaii. The only problem is that I'm terrified of flying and don't like boats. Can you fix it so that I can drive?"

"I'm sorry," replied the genie. "That would take too long, I'm afraid. Do you have a request for something a little easier?"

"Well, there is one other thing," said Plinkton. "I've always wanted to play scratch golf."

The genie thought for a moment. "Would you like that bridge to be two lanes or four?"

"Mind if I play through?"

"If you want to beat someone out on the golf course, just get him mad."

—*Dave Williams*

CALDWELL...

Herman and Patrick both sliced their drives into the rough then tromped through the high grass after them. As they searched high and low for the balls, a little old lady sat on her porch nearby watching them. The search had gone on for a few minutes before the lady spoke up.

"I hope I'm not interrupting your search," she said sweetly, "but would it be cheating if I told you where they are?"

DEFINITIONS

Cup sucker—ball rims around the hole a few times and does not fall.

Here's lookin' at you, kid—a bogey.

Rommel—hit from one sand trap into another sand trap.

On the dance floor but can't hear the music—the wrong side of a very large green.

Yank it and spank it—fast-play golf.

You played a little float on that shot—said to your partner when he skims a shot off a water hazard to safety.

Thank the monkeys—when your shot hits a tree and takes a good bounce.

Lauren, who was keeping score for the duo, said to her partner, "How'd you do on the par 3?"

"Not too bad," replied Jill. "I shot a 12."

"How in the world did you manage a 12 on a par 3?" asked Lauren.

"I sank a 30-foot putt."

"Every time I look at the ball, I see my ex-wife."

—*John Daly, explaining why he can hit a golf ball farther than anyone else on the pro tour*

Tina and Ben were playing in the annual husband-and-wife tournament at their local club. Ben was not really happy about playing with his spouse, but Tina insisted. By the time they reached the 13th tee, Ben's patience had been tested to the limit by his wife's constant talking to other couples in the tourney. While Ben prepared to hit his tee shot, Tina was at the ladies' tee talking and joking without a club in her hand. Ben decided to go ahead and tee off but, unfortunately, he misjudged his shot and hit his wife squarely in the back of the head, killing her instantly.

After her body was taken to the hospital, Doc Edwards came back to talk to Ben.

"We found a golf ball lodged three inches into the left side of her head, which was the cause of her death. However," he continued, "we found something else that really has us puzzled."

"What's that?" asked Ben.

"We also found another golf ball lodged three inches into her back."

"Oh, that," said Ben with a wave of his hand. "That was just my mulligan."

QUESTIONS

Q: What must a golfer shoot to assure tournament victory?

A: The rest of the field.

Q: Why is golf like fishing?

A: They both mysteriously encourage exaggeration.

Q: What is a golfer's least-favorite soft drink?

A: Slice.

Q: Who invented golf and said it was fun?

A: The same guy who invented bagpipes and said it was music.

Q: What's the difference between a whiff and a practice swing?

A: Nobody curses after a practice swing.

"Mulligan: invented by an Irishman who wanted to hit one more 20-yard grounder."

—*Jim Bishop*

A man from Chicago named McIntosh was on a business trip to the Near East. After working hard for two weeks, he decided to relax by playing a round of golf at the one course in the city. Being alone, he was paired up with three other players. McIntosh proceeded to play one of the worst rounds of his golfing career, which had been filled with many such rounds.

At the 15th green, he missed a ten-inch putt.

"$*%@#$!" he cried out as the ball lipped the cup, and he was forced to settle for another triple bogey. As the foursome began walking to the 16th tee, McIntosh turned toward his partners and with a smile said, "I wonder how you say '$*%@#$' in the local language?"

"That's easy," replied one of his playing partners. "Haven't you been listening to your caddy?"

Satan was holding a meeting in hell with all his little demons.

"You poor useless bunch of incompetents," he began. "There's much too much good in the world. You're supposed to be helping me spread evil, but instead you've just been wasting time and playing silly games. We need to make more people miserable." He stared out over them. "Now, what are you going to do about it?"

One small devil, new to the job, sheepishly raised his

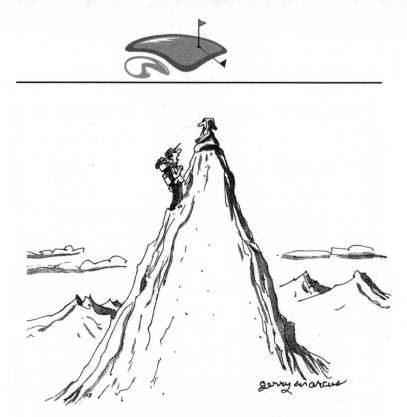

"That's it? Keep my head down?"

hand. "O, Lord of Darkness," he said, "I know I am not as knowledgeable as you, but may I make a suggestion?"

"Certainly," replied Satan.

"Well, Your Evilness, it seems to me that we could build people up and then knock them down," said the demon. "Their pain would then be even worse."

"Are you talking about golf?" asked another little demon.

"Steady, old man," Satan interrupted. "We just want to make them suffer. We don't want to finish them off in one shot."

GOLF IS . . .

90 percent inspiration and ten percent perspiration.

—Johnny Miller

a fine relief from the tensions of the office, but we are a little tired of holding the bag.

—Adlai Stevenson

an ideal diversion, but a ruinous disease.

—Bertie Charles Forbes

the hardest game in the world to play, and the easiest to cheat at.

—Dave Hill

like tennis. The game doesn't really start until the serves get in.

—Peter Thomson

Fenwick, a golfer on the PGA tour, died and went straight to hell. After some time, the devil noticed that Fenwick was not suffering like the rest of the souls. He checked the temperature gauge and saw that it was 95 degrees, with about 80 percent humidity. The devil went over to Fenwick and asked why he was so happy.

"Easy," said Fenwick. "The temperature and humidity are just like Florida in mid-March."

Not happy with that answer, the devil decided to make things a little bit rougher on the golfer. He went over to the controls and set the temperature at 105 degrees and the humidity at 90 percent.

A little later he checked back and, much to the devil's dismay, Fenwick still seemed as happy as could be. When asked why, Fenwick replied, "This is even better. Now it's like playing the Australian Open during December."

Now visibly upset, Satan vowed to show no mercy. He went to the controls and turned the heat up to 120 degrees. The humidity he raised to 100 percent. "Let's see how that golfer likes this!" he smiled.

When the devil found Fenwick sitting on the floor looking happier than ever, he was at a loss. He couldn't understand why the golfer was not suffering. He called Fenwick over and asked him. Fenwick replied, "This is great. It's just like playing in the U.S. Open!"

The devil stomped off in a rage. He promised himself that he would make the golfer suffer. Since heat hadn't worked he went to the controls and set the temperature to 25 degrees below zero. Within minutes the pools of molten lava splashing through hell began to turn to ice.

"Let's see how he likes it now," said Satan.

He looked around and found Fenwick jumping up and down with joy.

"Greg Norman has won the Masters!" he yelled. "Greg Norman has won the Masters!"

Banks hit his tee shot over toward the right side of the fairway, not far from where Albert, the greenskeeper, was walking. The ball missed him, but he was not happy that no one hollered "Fore!" when the ball had been hit. As Banks approached for his second shot, Albert confronted him.

"Hey, Mr. Banks," began Albert, "don't you know you're supposed to yell 'Fore!' to warn others that you hit your shot?"

"Sorry," said Banks, "but I didn't think it mattered since I knew it wasn't going to hit you."

"Wasn't going to hit me?" exclaimed Albert. "How could you be so sure?"

"Easy," answered Banks. "I was aiming right at you."

A deaf golfer named Peebles was out to play a round of golf all by himself, but he found himself more and more frustrated by the foursome ahead of him. They were taking extra shots, joking and fooling around, and generally wasting time. At the fifth tee, Peebles finally walked up to them to ask if they would mind if he played through. He wrote his request on a piece of paper and handed it to the fattest of the golfers. The man took the paper, read it out loud, and then laughed in Peebles's face. He then tore up the paper and tossed it away, and the foursome continued slowly with their round.

"Titleists are jucier, but Maxflis have more flavor."

By the seventh hole, Peebles was getting more and more irritated by the antics of the foursome. They had been wasting time, drinking from a container in their cart, and causing Peebles to spend most of the afternoon standing around. Fed up with all the procrastinating, he finally decided to do something about it.

He teed up his ball, and just as one of the foursome was getting ready to hit his second shot, Peebles hit his drive. The ball flew by the foursome, narrowly missing hitting one of them in the head. They turned around in anger and looked behind them. All they could see was Peebles holding up four fingers.

*"On second thought, that's too much club.
Better go with a woodwind."*

"Why do you play so much golf, Ben?" asked
Dolores, his disgusted wife.

Ben patted his ample stomach. "It keeps me in shape,"
he replied.

"In shape for what?" asked his incredulous wife.

"Golf."

"The income tax has made liars out of more
Americans than golf."

—*Will Rogers*

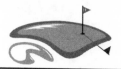

Belle, Booke, and Candelaria were out for their weekly round of golf at their country club. At the third hole, there was a lake right next to the green. On his fairway shot, Belle hit one right into the water, and the three friends rolled up their pant legs and waded into the water in search of the ball.

While searching, Candelaria happened to come upon an old lamp lying on the lake bottom. He took it out, and the three began to examine it.

Belle took out his handkerchief and rubbed the lamp. Sure enough, a puff of smoke came out of the lamp, and out popped a genie. The genie thanked the startled trio for releasing him from the lamp and, in exchange for his freedom, offered to grant a wish to each one of them.

"I wish I was wealthy," said Belle. Poof! When the smoke cleared, he looked around and found a pile of gold at his feet.

"I want to be attractive to women," said Booke. Poof! When the smoke cleared, he found his muscles starting to bulge under his shirt, and he grew taller. When he glanced into the water, a handsome face stared back.

Now it was Candelaria's turn. He thought for a moment, then announced, "I want to be God!" Poof! When the smoke dissipated, he found himself chairman of the rules committee.

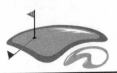

Burns and Allen, two golfers of approximately equal ability, were playing a round of golf together. They decided to "play it as it lays" on all shots.

At the first hole, both hit their shots straight down the middle, about 230 yards away. Burns hit his second shot down the middle once again, leaving the way for an easy approach shot to the green. Allen's second shot, however, sliced over the trees and wound up on the cart path of the adjoining hole.

"I guess I get a free drop from the cart path," said Allen.

"Oh, no," protested Burns. "We agreed to play every shot as it lays."

With that, Allen drove the golf cart up to Burns's ball in front of the green, and dropped Burns off. He then drove over to his ball on the gravel cart path.

As Burns watched in amusement, Allen took three or four practice swings on the cart path, sparks flying up each time his club came in contact with the gravel. Finally, Allen took his final swing and hit a perfect shot, and the ball came to rest on the green within five feet of the cup. Allen got back in the cart and drove up to the green.

"Wow!" marveled Burns. "That was a great shot you made, even if you screwed up your club. What club did you use?"

"Your 6-iron," replied Allen.

When the doctor answered the phone, a frantic voice on the other end of the line said, "Doctor! It's Parsons. We've got an emergency! My baby just swallowed my golf tees!"

"I'll be right over!" cried the doctor.

"But what should I do till you get here?" cried Parsons.

"Practice your putting."

After spending an afternoon playing a round of golf at his favorite resort in Cancún, Mexico, Albert returned to his suite to find his wife in the arms of the club's manager, Juan Escadero. While the surprised man hurriedly tried to put on his pants, an enraged Albert ran to his luggage, took out a gun, and shot the Latin lover. Escadero collapsed in a heap at the foot of the bed. The club's golf pro, who happened to be in the hall, heard the shot and rushed into the room. Taking in the situation at a glance, he walked over and clapped Albert on the back.

"Congratulations, señor!" he roared. "After all these years, you've finally made a hole in Juan!"

"A lot of guys who have never choked have never been in the position to do so."

—*Tom Watson*

Grande was out playing a round of golf at a neighborhood course. His caddy was Walters, an elderly man about 70 years of age. At the first tee, Grande hit his drive straight down the middle of the fairway.

"Oh, Mr. Grande," said Walters, "that was one of the finest shots I ever did see. Did I mention that I caddied for Jack Nicklaus last week on this course? He hit the very same shot in the very same place as you!"

Feeling pretty good, Grande walked down the fairway to his ball. Taking his 8-iron, he proceeded to hit the ball three feet from the cup.

"Mr. Grande," said Walters admiringly, "that was one of the finest shots I ever did see. Jack Nicklaus hit the very same shot in the very same place as you!"

His confidence now soaring, Grande holed out his putt for a birdie 3. He moved on to the second tee and blasted another drive straight down the middle.

"Wow, Mr. Grande," said Walters. "That was a fine shot. I have to say that when I caddied for Jack Nicklaus, he hit the very same shot in the very same place as you!"

Grande walked to his ball and eyed his approach shot to the green. Feeling pretty confident about himself, he turned to Walters and asked, "What club did Jack Nicklaus use for this shot?"

"Why, an 8-iron," replied Walters.

Grande took an 8-iron from Walters, lined up and hit the ball. It sailed into the air and fell about 30 yards short of the green.

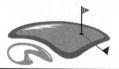

"I thought you said Jack Nicklaus hit an 8-iron on this shot," he said to Walters.

"He did," replied the old man.

"And where did Jack hit his shot?" asked Grande.

"About 30 yards short."

An American was golfing at Ireland's venerable Lahinch golf course for the first time, and playing absolutely terribly. After shanking yet another shot, he turned to the caddy and said, "This is absolutely amazing, Forrester. I've never played this badly before."

His caddy nodded. "Then, sir, you've played before?"

Grissom was playing alone at Pebble Beach one fine and beautiful day and was paired off with Cornfeld and Berry. After playing a few holes and getting to know each other, Cornfeld asked him why he was out playing such a beautiful course all by himself.

"Well, you see," replied Grissom, "my wife and I have played this course every year for the past twenty-five summers. However, she recently passed away. I'm keeping our tee time in her memory."

"That's very touching and sad," murmured Berry. "But I'd think you'd be able to find a friend to take her place."

"So did I," replied Grissom. "But they all wanted to go to her funeral."

Glock was a con man, always on the lookout for a
new way to make money. One fall, he came up with
the idea of teaching a gorilla to play golf. Dollar signs
flashed through his mind as he pictured himself getting
rich with this unique attraction. He purchased a gorilla
from a circus and spent the entire winter teaching him
how to play golf. By the time spring rolled around, he
was ready to begin making money. He went to a local
golf course and bet the club pro $5,000 that his gorilla
could beat the pro in a round of golf. The pro quickly
accepted the bet.

On the first hole, a long par 5, the pro teed up and
hit his drive 275 yards straight down the middle of the
fairway. The gorilla then proceeded to slam his ball
some 500 yards to within just a few feet of the hole.

"That's unbelievable," marveled the pro. "There's no
way I'm going to be able to beat this gorilla." He gave
up and handed Glock his money.

Over the next couple of weeks, the same scenario
was carried out at golf courses around the country.
Every golfer matched against the gorilla gave up after
seeing the opening 500-yard drive.

Now Glock was ready for the big time. He contacted
Ernie Els about a match. The round was arranged, but
this time the bet was for $100,000.

The day of the big match, Els teed up at the first hole
and hit his drive 300 yards right down the center of the

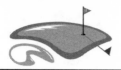

fairway. The gorilla stepped up to the tee and drove the ball 500 yards right down the middle. It landed on the green only ten feet away from the cup.

Els shook his head in amazement but did not give up. He hit a magnificent second shot to within 20 feet of the pin, then putted out for an eagle.

The gorilla took out his putter, paced off his putt, and stepped up to the ball. He then hit it 500 yards.

"Every time my wife takes the car there's trouble. The other day she came home, there were 100 dents in the car. She said she took a shortcut through a driving range."

—*Rodney Dangerfield*

Kelsey was sitting in the clubhouse bar stirring his drink and reflecting on the consequences of his most recent extramarital affair. Deep in thought, he absent-mindedly began talking to himself.

"It's not worth it," he muttered out loud. "It's never as good as you hope. It's expensive and, above all else, it drives your wife berserk."

A friend who was sitting close by overheard Kelsey's words. He leaned across and said, "Don't complain, Kelsey. You knew what to expect when you took up golf."

"The greatest liar in the world is the golfer who claims he plays the game merely for exercise."

—*Tommy Bolt*

An avid golfer named Newell died and ended up at the pearly gates of heaven, where he was greeted by St. Peter.

"Would you like to look around?" asked the celestial gatekeeper. Newall assented and was given a tour of heaven.

"Very lovely," commented Newell after they had been walking a while. "Everyone seems happy, and your place is beautiful, but tell me, where are the golf courses?"

"We've had that question asked before," replied Peter. "Especially by the folks who have arrived in the last three or four hundred years. Maybe we'll get around to building some in a few thousand years, but we just don't have any at present."

A disgusted Newell waved his hand and headed for the exit. Outside the gate was an elevator with only one stop indicated. Newell stepped inside, pushed "Down" and moments later was in hell, where he was met by the devil.

"Just one question," said Newell. "Do you have any golf courses?"

"Of course," grinned the devil. "Let me show you."

"I'm being married right this minute by proxy."

Newell was astonished as the devil showed him course after course, each more beautiful than the one before. He couldn't wait to play.

"Do you have any clubs and balls?" asked an eager Newell. "I'm ready to join up."

"I'm afraid not," the evil one replied, grinning.

"A dozen beautiful courses like this—how could you not have any clubs and balls?"

"That's right, no equipment," said the devil. "That's the hell of it."

GOLF IS. . .

a game where you take a ball about an inch across, and put it on a ball several thousand miles across. The idea is to hit the little ball.

a game in which a little white ball is chased around by men too old to chase anything else.

a rich man's sport that has millions of poor players.

an expensive way of playing marbles.

a game in which the slowest people in the world are those in front of you, and the fastest are those behind.

a five-mile walk punctuated by disappointments.

as life; you strive for the green, but end up in the hole.

a game where the ball lies poorly, and the players well.

an easy game. It's just hard to play.

a game where you start out with three friends, play 18 holes, and return with three enemies.

a game in which you match your skill against your opponent's luck.

"Are you my caddy today?" asked Buckley.

"Yes, sir."

"Are you good at finding lost balls?" Buckley asked.

"Yes, sir. I find every lost ball."

"Good. Run and look for one so we can start."

Turning to her caddy, Barbara said, "Would you mind wading into the lake and retrieving my ball?"

"Why?"

"It's my lucky ball."

"I play with friends, but we don't play friendly games."

—*Ben Hogan*

A husband and wife were on the eighth green when a ball came whizzing through, almost striking the man. His startled wife looked back and saw another couple some 150 yards in back of them.

"Hey, you jerk!" she yelled. "You almost hit my husband."

"I'm terribly sorry!" the woman yelled back. "Here, have a shot at mine."

"How would you have played that last shot?" Smith asked his caddy.

"Under an assumed name."

"Competitive golf is played mainly on a five-and-a-half-inch course: the space between your ears."

—*Bobby Jones*

Lucy, Jenna, Georgia, and Meg returned to the club-house after an afternoon of golf.

"How did your game go?" asked the club pro.

"Great," replied Lucy. "I had a terrific round with 25 riders."

"Very good," said Jenna. "I did pretty well with 18 riders."

"Okay," allowed Georgia. "I didn't do too badly, with 12 riders."

"Not too good," admitted Meg. "I only had four riders the entire round."

A bit confused, but not wanting to sound ignorant because he didn't know what a rider was, the pro smiled and wished them better luck the next time. After they left, however, he approached Joe the bartender and asked, "Joe, can you tell me what in the world a rider is?"

"Sure," said Joe, smiling. "A rider is when you have hit a shot long enough to take a ride on a golf cart."

A duffer named Barbara was just finishing up her lesson with the club pro, and her frustration was showing. As she shanked one drive after another, she was swearing and muttering under her breath.

"I'm afraid you're not addressing the ball correctly," instructed the pro.

"Listen," snarled Barbara. "I was polite with it for as long as possible!"

Murvay had just finished a round of golf and went into the club bar to have a beer. There he ran into his friend Woodruff. "Hey, Woody. Didn't know you were here today. Who'd you play with?"

"I played with a new member named Forrester," replied Woodruff. "Nice guy, and practically ready for the PGA tour."

"Really! That good?"

"Oh, yes! He was hitting nearly 300 yards off the tee. Straight down the middle every time. Long iron shots and never in trouble. Read the greens like David Duval. Never three-putted."

"Wow," said an impressed Murvay. "He sounds like a great player. You must've lost pretty badly."

"No, I won!"

Bumper sticker: "If you think I'm a lousy driver, wait until you see me putt."

Phillip and Morris were walking up to the 18th hole, a short par 3. Phillip had played his best round ever, but luck certainly had been on his side. Every bounce had gone his way. On the third hole, his tee shot had been heading out of bounds when it struck a tree and caromed back into the middle of the fairway. On the sixth hole, his drive had hit the cart path, continued bouncing along, and came to rest just short of the greenside bunker. On the 13th green, his long putt had ricocheted off a tiny pebble and gone right into the cup for a birdie.

Morris, on the other hand, could not have been doing much worse. Dame Fortune had her back to him all afternoon. He had been in and out of half the bunkers on the course and had three short putts just lip the cup. Needless to say, Morris was not in the best of moods as Phillip teed up on 18.

Even though a stiff wind was blowing in his face, Phillip still managed to hit his shot perfectly, right down the middle, landing about ten feet from the cup.

"What did you hit?" asked Morris, trying to sound casual.

"A 3," responded Phillip with a smile.

Not to be outdone, Morris pulls out his 3-iron. He pounded his ball 35 yards over the green and into the lake beyond.

"Didn't you just hit a 3-iron?" he asked incredulously.

"No," purred his friend. "A Titleist Number Three."

A foursome was just putting out on the ninth hole when another golfer came running up. Almost out of breath, the man gasped, "Do you mind if I play through? I've just gotten word that my wife has taken seriously ill."

Pendleton had spent most of the morning arguing with his caddy on almost every shot about which club to hit, and on every shot his caddy's opinion had been proven correct. Finally, on the 16th hole, a 195-yard par 3 into the wind, his caddy handed him his 4-wood. Seething by this time, Pendleton hesitated.

"I think it's a 3-iron," said Pendleton.

"Nope," said his caddie. "It's a 4-wood."

"I disagree," repeated Pendleton. "It's definitely a 3-iron."

Deciding to show his caddy who was boss, Pendleton took out his 3-iron and hit a perfect shot which sliced through the wind, hit the front of the green, and rolled five feet short of the cup.

As a smug Pendleton began walking down the fairway, his caddy said, "See, I told you it wasn't enough club."

"Most golfers prepare for disaster. A good golfer prepares for success."

—*Bob Toski*

The local bishop and a county judge were teamed up at the country club for golf. The two were playing to the same handicap and were evenly matched through 15 holes.

The judge hit his approach shot to the edge of the green while the bishop's shot landed in the sand trap next to the green. The judge watched as his friend anchored his feet and wiggled the sand wedge in his hands before taking a mighty swing. Sand went everywhere, but the ball moved not an inch. The bishop stared at the ball for a full minute, his head quivering.

Finally, the judge interrupted. "That was the most profane silence I have ever witnessed."

Allison and Killebrew were out golfing one fine day. At the eighth hole, Allison sliced his tee shot deep into a wooded ravine that bordered the fairway. He took an 8-iron with him and climbed down into the ravine to look for his ball. After hacking around in the brush for a few minutes, he noticed something shiny. Moving closer, he realized it was an 8-iron clutched in the hands of a skeleton which was lying next to a very old golf ball. Allison excitedly called out to his friend, "Hey, Killebrew, I've got a problem down here."

Killebrew ran over to the edge of the ravine and looked down, "What's the matter, Allison?"

"Toss me down my 7-iron," hollered Allison. "You can't get out of here with an 8!"

Gena was out playing a round of golf and was paired up with a priest. On the seventh hole, the priest turned to her and asked, "What club are you going to use on this hole, young lady?"

"An 8-iron, Father," answered Gena. "How about you?"

The priest pondered for a moment. "I think I'm going to hit a soft 7-iron and pray."

Gena proceeded to hit her 8-iron and put the ball on the green. The priest then topped his 7-iron shot and dribbled the ball out a few yards.

"I wonder how that happened," grumbled the priest.

"Well, I don't know about you, Father," said Gena, "but in my church, when we pray we keep our heads down."

In the clubhouse after another afternoon of slices, shanks, and blown putts, Morganstern was looking for any words of encouragement.

"Well, Jonesy," he said, addressing his caddy, "did I look any better out there today?"

"Yes sir, Mr. Morganstern," replied Jonesy. "Those new golf pants make you look much better."

"The golf swing is like sex. You can't be thinking about the mechanics of the act while you are performing."

—*Dave Hill*

"It's nice to have the opportunity to play for so much money, but it's nicer to win it."

—Patty Sheenan

"As you walk down the fairway of life you must smell the roses, for you only get to play one round."

—Ben Hogan

Three Orthodox rabbis, dressed in black and with long black beards, were out for an afternoon of golf. O'Hanlon, playing by himself, was paired up with them. At the end of 18 holes, O'Hanlon's score was 107, while the rabbis carded a 70, 70, and 71.

"How did you become such good players?" asked O'Hanlon.

"When you live a religious life and you attend temple regularly," explained the first rabbi, "you are rewarded."

O'Hanlon pondered this for a minute. Since he loved golf above all else, he figured he had nothing to lose. He went home and found a synagogue in his neighborhood. After attending services twice every week, he converted and began to live a holy life, attending religious services regularly.

About a year later, he happened to again meet up with the same three rabbis on the golf course. He joined them for a round, and at the end of the day, his score again was 107, while the rabbis' scores were 70, 70, and 71.

"For some reason people lose a lot of balls on this hole."

"I don't understand," he sighed. "I did everything you said. I joined a temple, attended services regularly, and have led a holy life. How come I'm still playing so badly?"

"Hmmm," mused the eldest of the rabbis. "What temple did you join?"

"Beth Shalom," replied O'Hanlon.

"There's your mistake!" the rabbi said. "Beth Shalom is for tennis!"

93

Annie walked into her bedroom and was greeted by the unusual sight of Patrick in bed with his golf clubs. "What are you doing?" asked the astonished wife.

"Gee," said Patrick, "I don't know why you're so surprised. Didn't you say I had to choose?"

The duffer named Larkin turned to his caddy and said, "This is my first day playing golf. When do I use my putter?"

The caddy rolled his eyes. "Hopefully, sometime before dark."

"In today's modern world, the American businessman spends all morning talking about golf in his office. The rest of his day he spends discussing work on the golf course."

—*Anonymous*

As Larry headed out the door, he had his bag of clubs clutched in his hand. His wife yelled after him, "You're going to get fired if you don't go into the office once in a while."

"It's okay, hon," Larry yelled back. "The HMO said I had to take my iron every day."

"If there is any larceny in man, golf will bring it out."

—Unknown

Two woman were having lunch at the golf club, and one had been telling the other about a trip abroad that she and her husband had just taken.

"It sounds wonderful," said the second. "While you were overseas did you go to the Holy Land?"

"Oh, yes," said the first. "My husband insisted that we go to St. Andrews."

After she sliced a long drive into the woods, Anderson was upset when she couldn't find the ball.

"Caddy," she said with a sarcastic sneer, "why didn't you see where that ball went?"

"You caught me off guard," replied her caddy. "It usually doesn't go anywhere."

Little Bobby was telling the rest of the family about having walked around the course with his father for the first time.

"My daddy's the best golfer in the whole world," he exclaimed proudly. "He can play for hours and hardly ever let the ball get in those little holes."

"Several times in the 1980s,
he walked around a golf course."